I0606072

The POWER of Her PAINTBRUSH

The Story of THERESA BERNSTEIN

by JANICE HECHTER

KAR-BEN PUBLISHING

From the time she drew her first portrait of her friend Lorena at age seven, Theresa never stopped making art. She was constantly sketching and painting.

One day at school, thirteen-year-old Theresa was standing at the blackboard when the principal introduced a guest to her class: Dr. Blackwood, who had served in the Civil War. With a stick of chalk, Theresa quickly created his portrait on the blackboard. Her teacher and classmates were amazed.

Theresa had a photographic memory, which came in handy. Whenever she stumbled upon something that she wanted to paint, she made a quick sketch and headed home to paint from memory.

At age seventeen, Theresa headed to the Philadelphia School of Design for Women to study art. She won many prizes there, but it wasn't always easy.

Once, after pouring much time and effort into a painting, Theresa entered it in a competition. Visiting the exhibit space the night before the show, she tingled with delight at the thought of seeing her work on a gallery wall. But what she saw when she entered the gallery outraged her.

Someone had splashed ink on her painting so she wouldn't win a prize.

Theresa grabbed her damaged painting and raced out the door.

Determined to have a painting in the competition, Theresa stayed up and painted all night.

She turned in her new painting the next day and won FIRST PRIZE!

After graduating from art school, Theresa moved to New York City—to Manhattan, the center of the art world. An adviser from art school had given her the name of a woman artist who might be able to help Theresa with her career.

"Take my advice and study typing," the artist told Theresa, knowing how hard it was for women to be successful in an art world that favored men.

The words stung, but Theresa was determined to succeed. She had many ideas and was eager to transfer them onto canvas. She enrolled in painting classes so she could keep improving her skills. With the little money she had to spare, she rented a tiny art studio that had no windows and no heat.

Theresa brought some of her paintings to an art store to be framed. The shop owner liked her work so much that he bought a few pieces. And he had an idea for Theresa.

He suggested that she submit a painting to an exhibition at the National Academy of Design.

The academy chose one of Theresa's paintings, *Open-Air Show*, for the exhibition.

The exhibit moved on to major museums in Pittsburgh and Chicago. When an English art collector spotted Theresa's painting, he purchased it and became one of her biggest fans. This connection later led to a glowing review of Theresa's work in an important art journal.

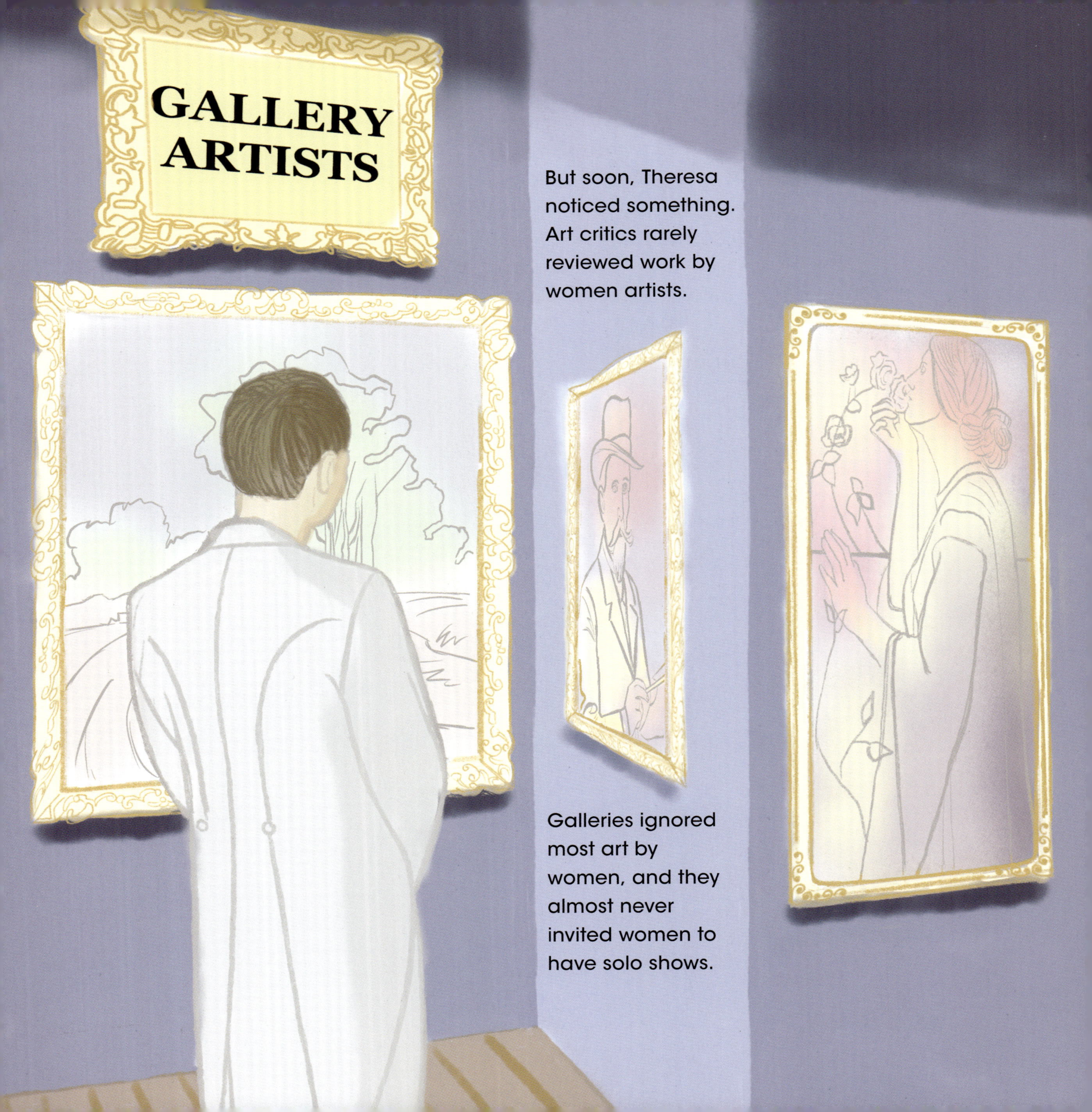

But soon, Theresa noticed something. Art critics rarely reviewed work by women artists.

Galleries ignored most art by women, and they almost never invited women to have solo shows.

Contest juries awarded almost all their prizes to men. This also made it harder for women to sell their artwork, since most people only wanted to buy art from well-known, respected artists.

Many men grumbled at the idea of including women in art shows. Some art galleries held group shows of "women's artwork," but this label made women's art seem less important and less impressive than men's.

T. Bernstein
T. Bernstein

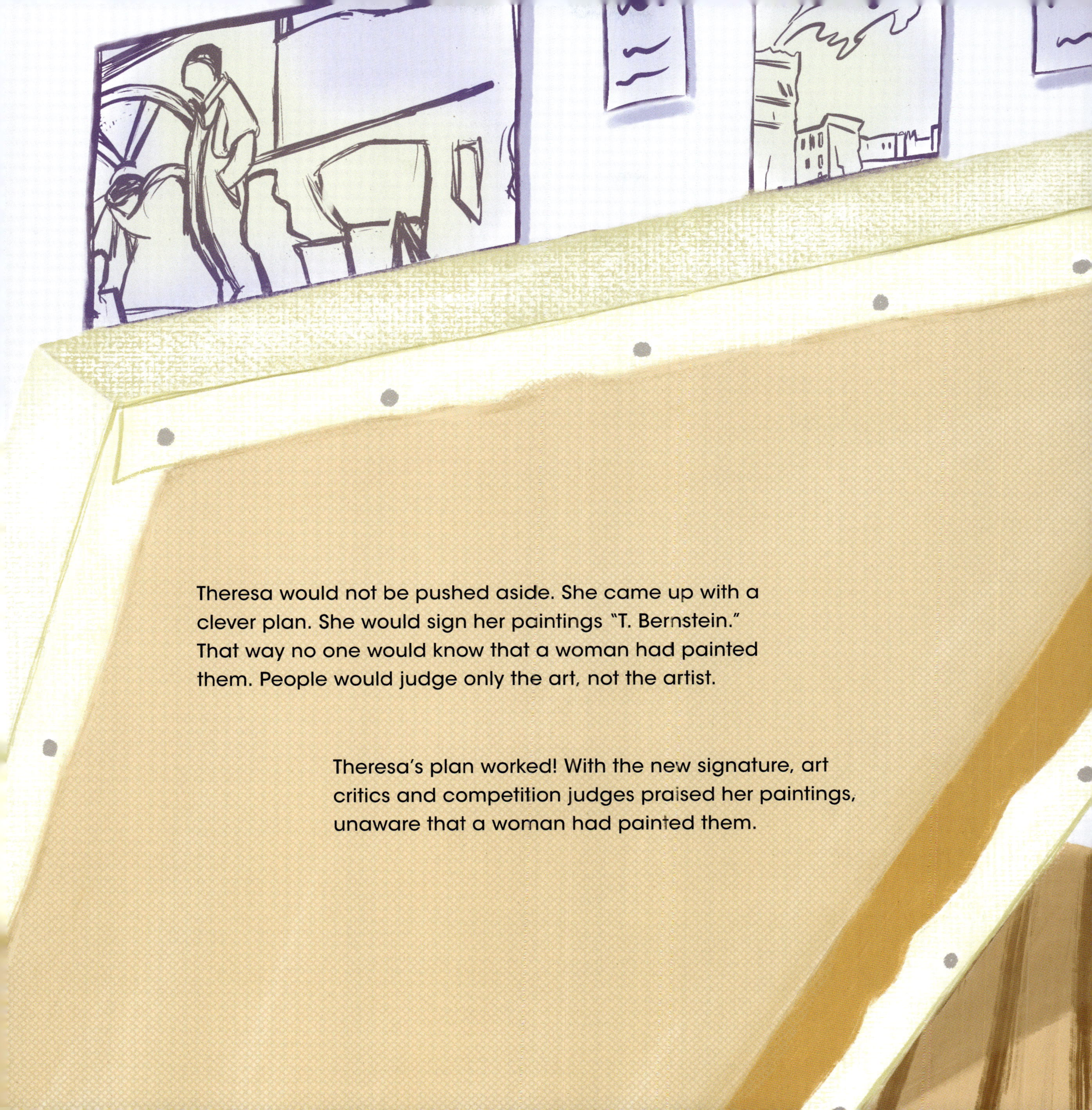

Theresa would not be pushed aside. She came up with a clever plan. She would sign her paintings "T. Bernstein." That way no one would know that a woman had painted them. People would judge only the art, not the artist.

Theresa's plan worked! With the new signature, art critics and competition judges praised her paintings, unaware that a woman had painted them.

Wherever she went, Theresa sketched. She drew on anything she could get her hands on, even restaurant tablecloths, napkins, and menus.

Theresa painted every day.

She swept her canvases with breezy brushstrokes.

Her paintings brimmed with raging reds, spicy oranges, cinnamon browns, and sunflower yellows.

In 1914, when women were fighting for the right to vote, Theresa slipped into the night and sketched the crowds at suffragist meetings and parades. Unlike many male artists, who painted women as delicate and decorative, Theresa painted real-life women, filled with hopes, struggles, and dreams.

ES FOR
VOTES FOR WOMEN
EQUALITY FOR WOMEN
VOTES FOR
Give us the vote NOW

Theresa had always been fascinated with beaches. She planned a painting trip to Gloucester, Massachusetts, where sandy shorelines, brilliant sunlight, and vivid colors dotted the landscape.

But Gloucester did not welcome Jews. After her long train ride from New York, none of the inns in the area would give her a room because she was Jewish.

Theresa refused to turn back. She met an artist who offered to let her stay in his attic. Once settled in, Theresa scurried to the seashore to paint.

One day, a group of men visited Theresa's studio.

"We have come to see your father," one of them said. "We want to invite him to become a member of the Salmagundi Club."

Theresa knew this was the oldest and most prestigious art club in New York.

When they found out that she—not her father—was the artist, the men harrumphed and left.

Word soon spread that "T. Bernstein" was a woman.

But by now, Theresa's work had been noticed by gallery owners and art critics. People had recognized her talent. Her plan had paid off.

SOLD

SOLD

In 1919, at age twenty-nine, Theresa got a chance to do something that was out of reach for most women artists of the time. She was given a one-woman art exhibit for her work at the Milch Gallery in New York City. She sold ten paintings on opening day!

The *New York Herald*'s glowing review of Theresa's show said, "It is with a man's vision that this artist looks at her subjects." The writer had meant this as a compliment!

Theresa firmly believed that it was her view of the world *as a woman* that made her paintings so powerful. She continued to paint what moved her, and she continued to display and sell her work in one-woman shows.

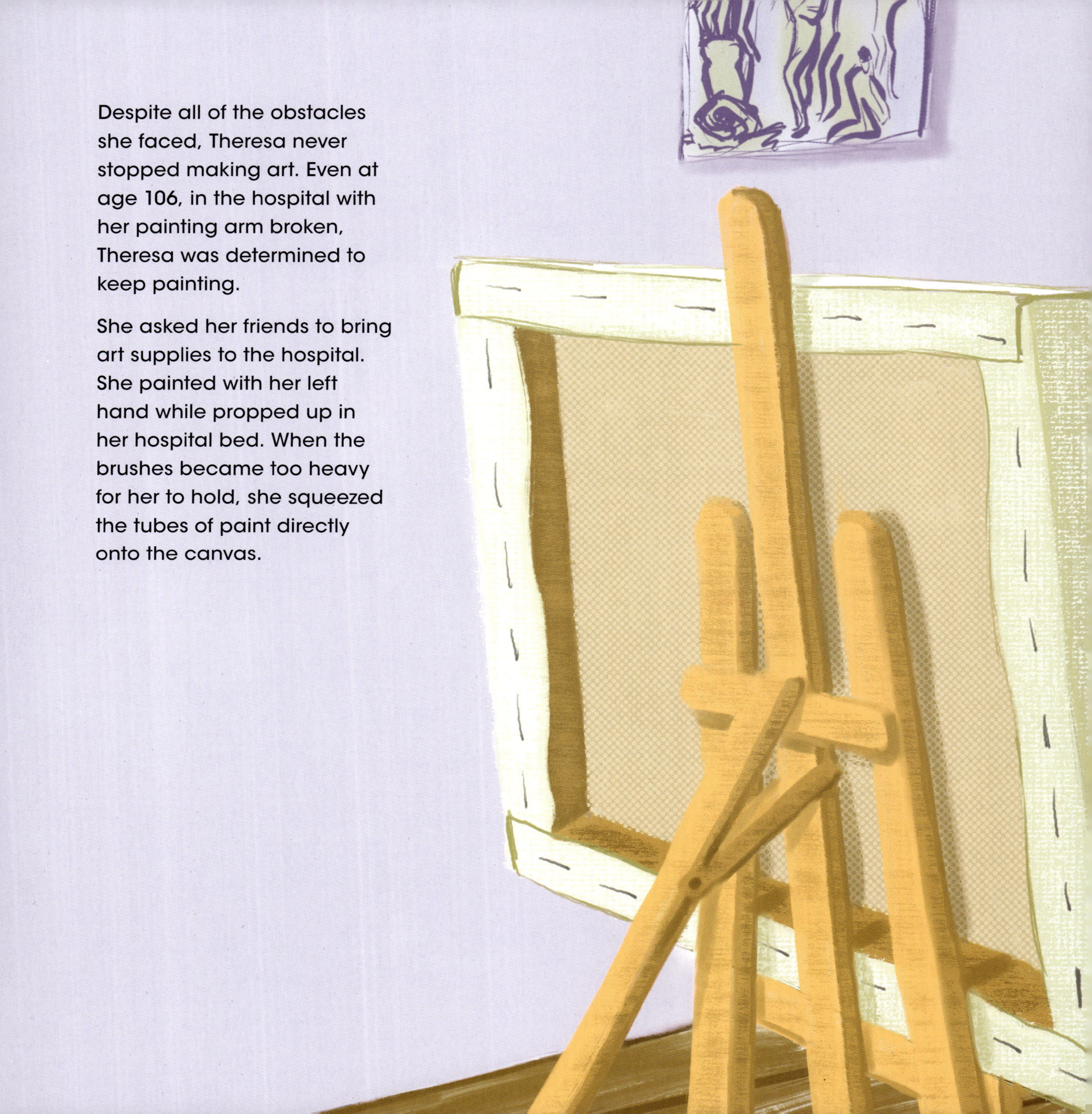

Despite all of the obstacles she faced, Theresa never stopped making art. Even at age 106, in the hospital with her painting arm broken, Theresa was determined to keep painting.

She asked her friends to bring art supplies to the hospital. She painted with her left hand while propped up in her hospital bed. When the brushes became too heavy for her to hold, she squeezed the tubes of paint directly onto the canvas.

Theresa Bernstein continued to make remarkable art until the age of 110. Even today, Theresa's legacy lives on, inspiring new generations of artists with the power of her paintbrush.

Author's Note

Theresa Bernstein was an American artist, born in Kraków, in what is now Poland, and raised in Philadelphia, Pennsylvania. She was born in 1890, just before the turn of the twentieth century.

She achieved great success and recognition, despite living at a time of inequality for women. Theresa's paintings are included in permanent art collections across the country, including the Metropolitan Museum of Art, the Art Institute of Chicago, the Brooklyn Museum, the Phillips Collection, the Smithsonian National Museum of American Art, the New York Public Library, the Library of Congress, the Cape Ann Museum, Harvard University, and the National Gallery of Art.

Unusual for a woman of her day, Theresa showed her paintings in more than forty one-woman exhibitions. She painted the important events of every decade, from suffragists rallying for women's voting rights in the early 1900s to hippies gathering in Central Park in the 1960s. In the 1970s and 1980s, she painted scenes of basketball players, fascinated by their ballet-like movements. Also in the 1980s, she captured the kicks, twists, turns, and spins of breakdancers.

In 1998, at age 108, Theresa had a one-woman show at Joan Whalen Fine Art, a New York gallery. Clapping and waving fans swooped in as TV cameras filmed Theresa entering the gallery. People formed lines down 57th Street, waiting for their chance to meet the artist.

Theresa Bernstein died in 2002, just two weeks shy of her 112th birthday.

Artist Theresa Bernstein standing in front of one of her paintings in 1924

New England Ladies, by Theresa Bernstein, c. 1925, on exhibit in the Cape Ann Museum, Gloucester, Massachusetts

Self Portrait of the Artist, by Theresa Bernstein, c. 1920, on exhibit in the Cape Ann Museum, Glouchester, Massachusetts

For Dara Hechter, Girard (Jerry) Jackson, Keith Carlson, Michele Cohen, Diane M. Dawson, and Sylvia Selfridge, who all helped make this book a reality.

KAR-BEN PUBLISHING®
An imprint of Lerner Publishing Group, Inc.
241 First Avenue North
Minneapolis, MN 55401 USA
Website address: www.karben.com

Additional image credits: Library of Congress, p. 31(top); paintings by Theresa Bernstein courtesy of Wikimedia Commons, PD, p. 31.

Main body text set in ITC Avant Garde Gothic
Typeface provided by Adobe Systems.

Library of Congress Cataloging-in-Publication Data

Names: Hechter, Janice author illustrator
Title: The power of her paintbrush : the story of Theresa Bernstein / by Janice Hechter ; illustrated by Janice Hechter.
Description: Minneapolis : Kar-Ben Publishing, [2026] | includes biographical information | Audience: Ages 5–9 | Audience: Grades K–1 | Summary: "Theresa Bernstein started drawing at seven and honed her talent at the Philadelphia School of Design. In New York, she used "T. Bernstein" to gain recognition in a male-dominated art world, paving the way for future female artists"— Provided by publisher.
Identifiers: LCCN 2025009699 (print) | LCCN 2025009700 (ebook) | ISBN 9798765643273 library binding | ISBN 9798765693711 epub
Subjects: LCSH: Bernstein, Theresa—Juvenile literature | Painters—United States—Biography—Juvenile literature | Women painters—United States—Biography—Juvenile literature | LCGFT: Biographies
Classification: LCC ND237.B54 H43 2026 (print) | LCC ND237.B54 (ebook) | DDC 759.13 [B]—dc23/eng/20250519

LC record available at https://lccn.loc.gov/2025009699
LC ebook record available at https://lccn.loc.gov/2025009700

Manufactured in Guang Dong, China by Dream Colour Printing
1-1012631-52382-5/12/2025